THE HANDMADE COUNTING BOOK

Laura Rankin

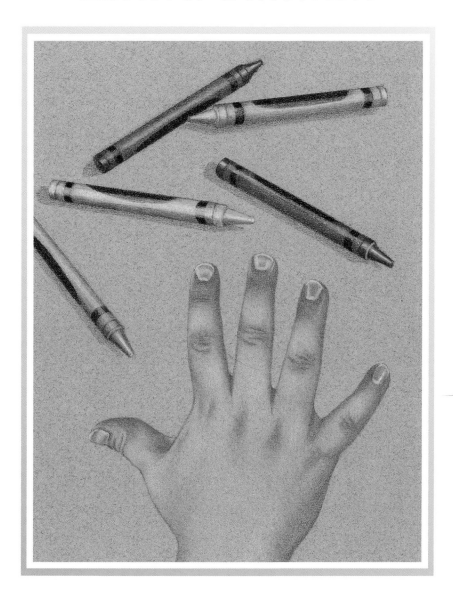

DIAL BOOKS NEW YORK

For Ed
my brother
with love

❧

Grateful thanks to Mary Beth Miller and Lou Ann Walker for
their expert assistance in checking the Artist's Note and pictures for accuracy,
and to Mary Catherine Hess for her contribution to the description of ASL.

Published by Dial Books
A member of Penguin Putnam Inc.
375 Hudson Street
New York, New York 10014

Copyright © 1998 by Laura Rankin
All rights reserved • Designed by Nancy R. Leo
Printed in Hong Kong
First Edition
1 3 5 7 9 10 8 6 4 2

Library of Congress Cataloging in Publication Data
Rankin, Laura.
The handmade counting book / Laura Rankin.—1st ed.
p.   m.
Summary: Shows how to count from one to twenty and twenty-five, fifty,
seventy-five, and one hundred using American Sign Language.
ISBN 0-8037-2309-1 (trade). — ISBN 0-8037-2311-3 (lib. bdg.)
1. Finger spelling—United States—Juvenile literature.
2. Counting—Juvenile literature. [1. Sign language. 2. Counting.] I. Title.
HV2477.R363 1998   419—dc21   97-38463   CIP   AC

The art for each picture consists of colored pencil on charcoal paper.

Artist's Note

The Handmade Counting Book shows how to count using American Sign Language (ASL), a language used by most Deaf people in the United States and English-speaking parts of Canada. Family, friends, and teachers who are not Deaf also use ASL. Like all languages, ASL has its own grammar and rules that are unique to the language. Each sign is based on the shape, movement, and position of the hand, as well as where the sign is made—near the face or touching an arm, for instance.

When you meet Deaf people, you'll see that some use slightly different signs for a few of the numbers shown in this book. There is more than one way to sign certain numbers.

How to Look at the Pictures

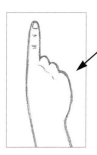

Here is an example of the way the numbers are signed in this book.

When you look at a sign, imagine that someone is signing the number to you, like this.

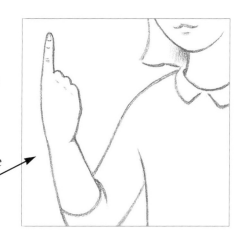

Hand and Finger Movement

The signs for the numbers 10-100 involve movement of the hand. Here is how these signs are shown in the book.

 1. Lightly drawn hand shows the start position.

 2. An arrow points to the next movement, shown by the more solidly drawn hand.

 3. Double lines above an arrow mean you move your hand back and forth, or up and down, several times in the direction of the lines. Here's an example:

1. Start position.

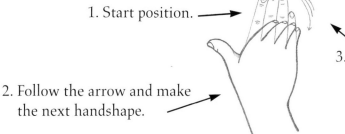

3. Move fingers up and down several times. You just signed the number 15!

2. Follow the arrow and make the next handshape.

1

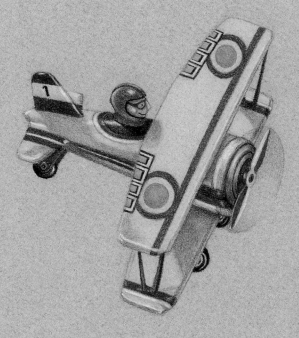

3

5

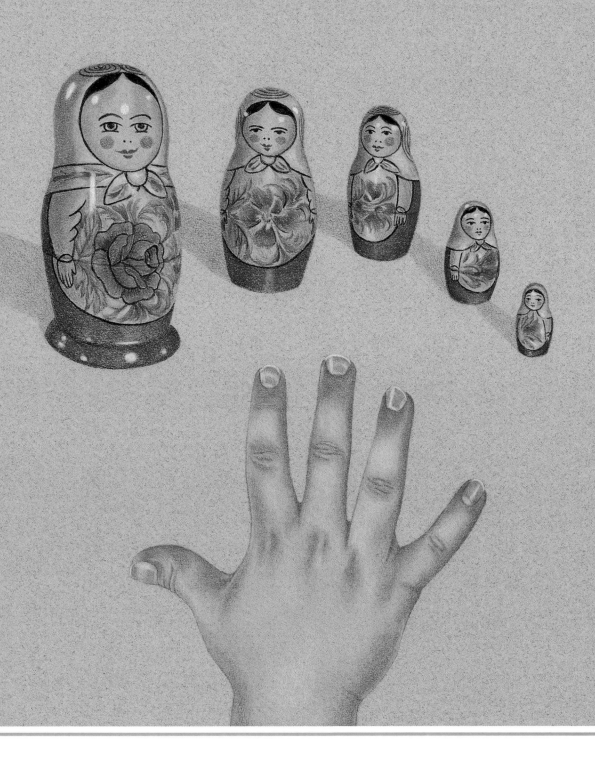

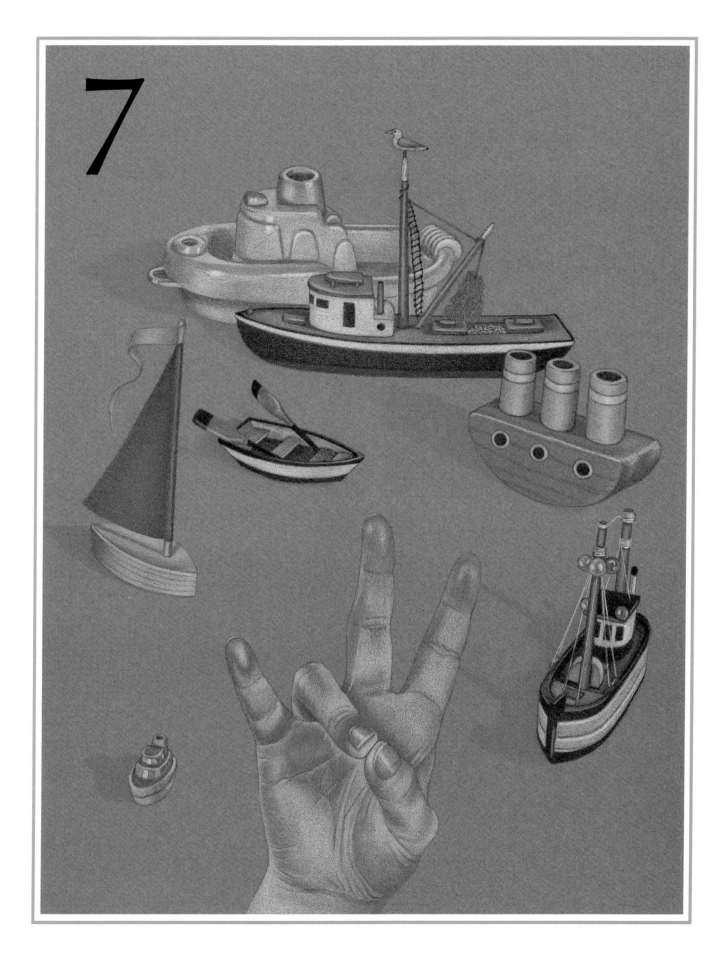

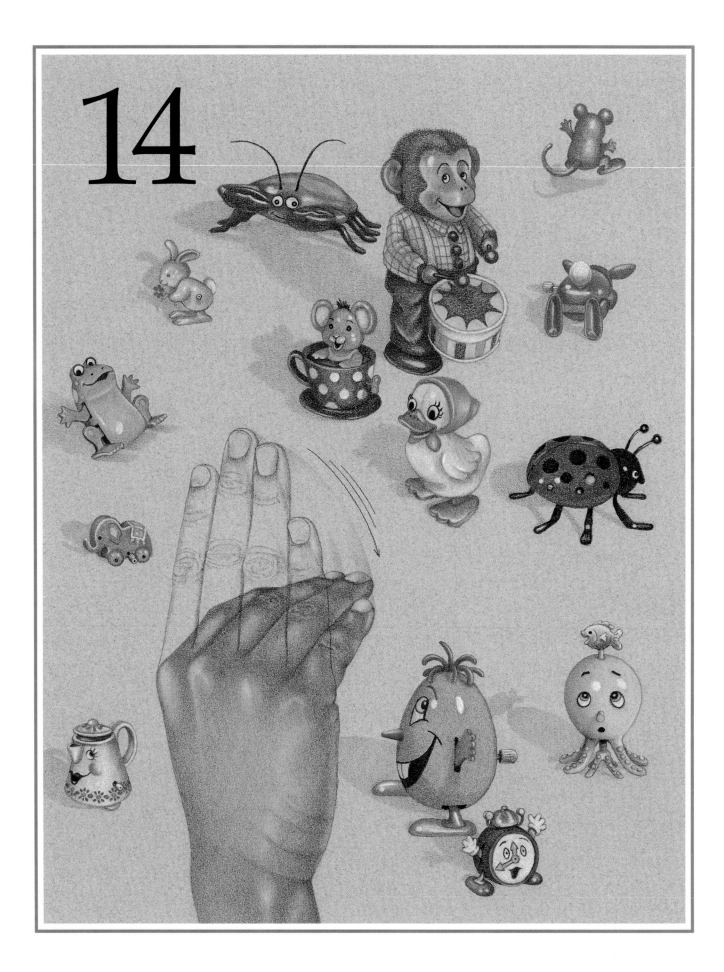

16

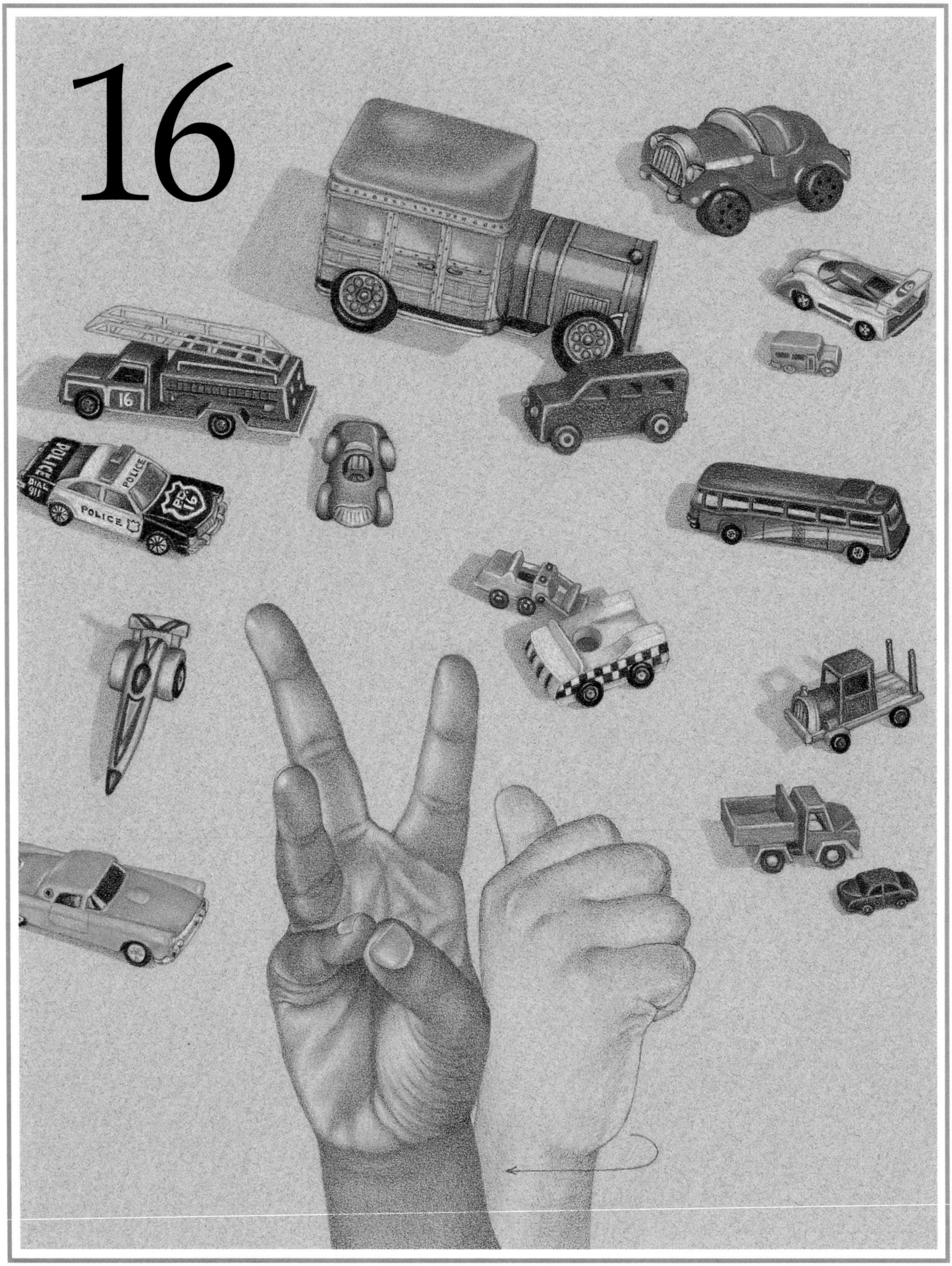

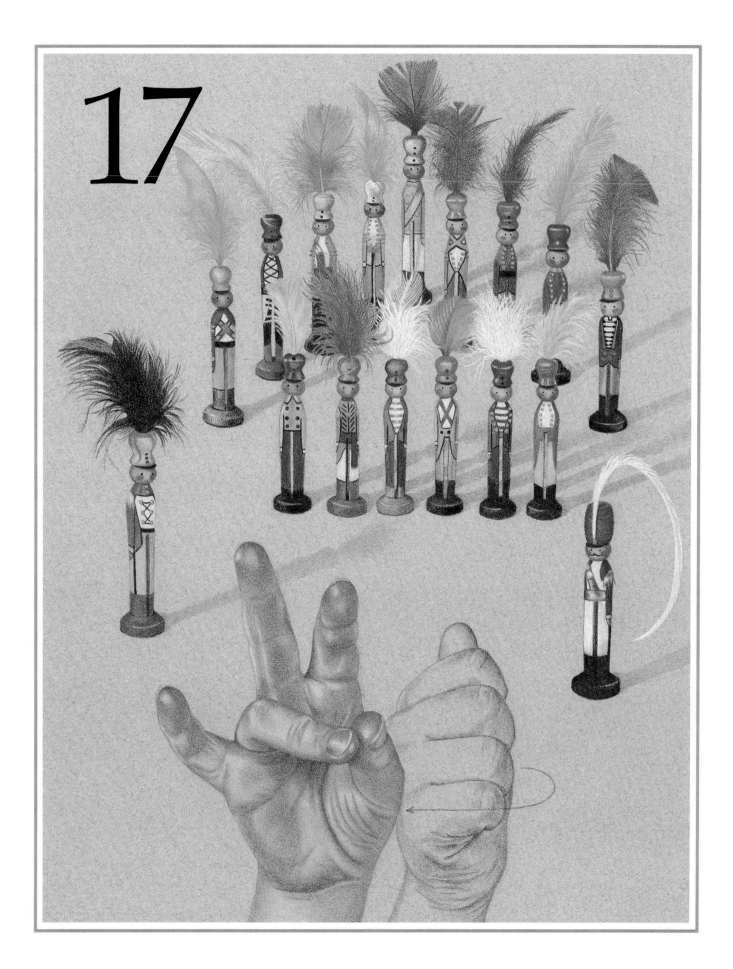

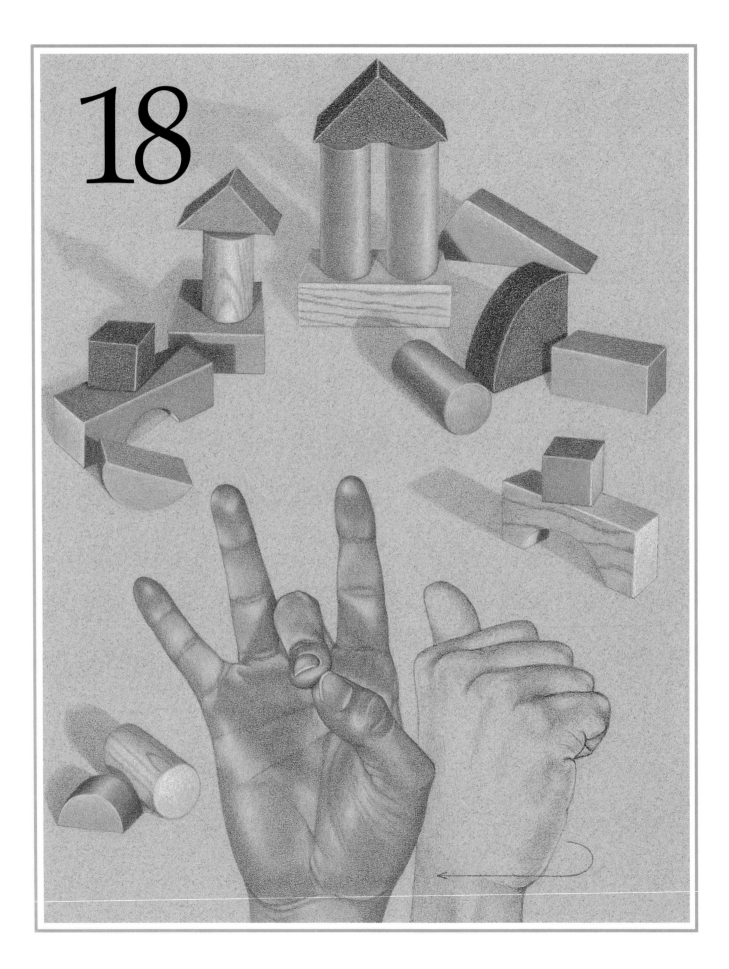

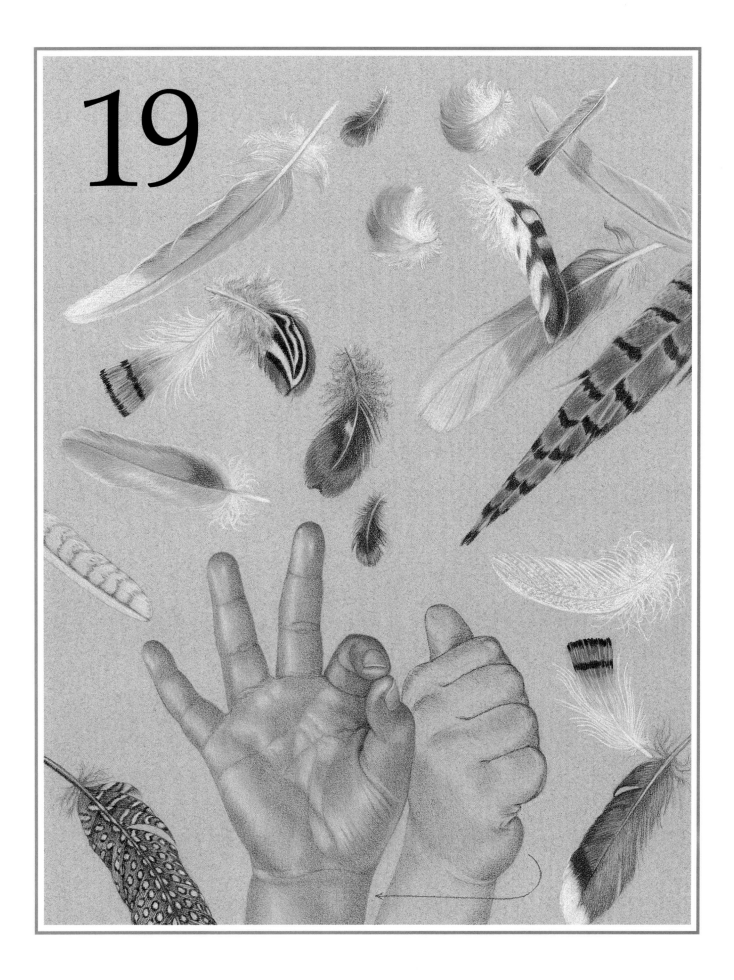

20

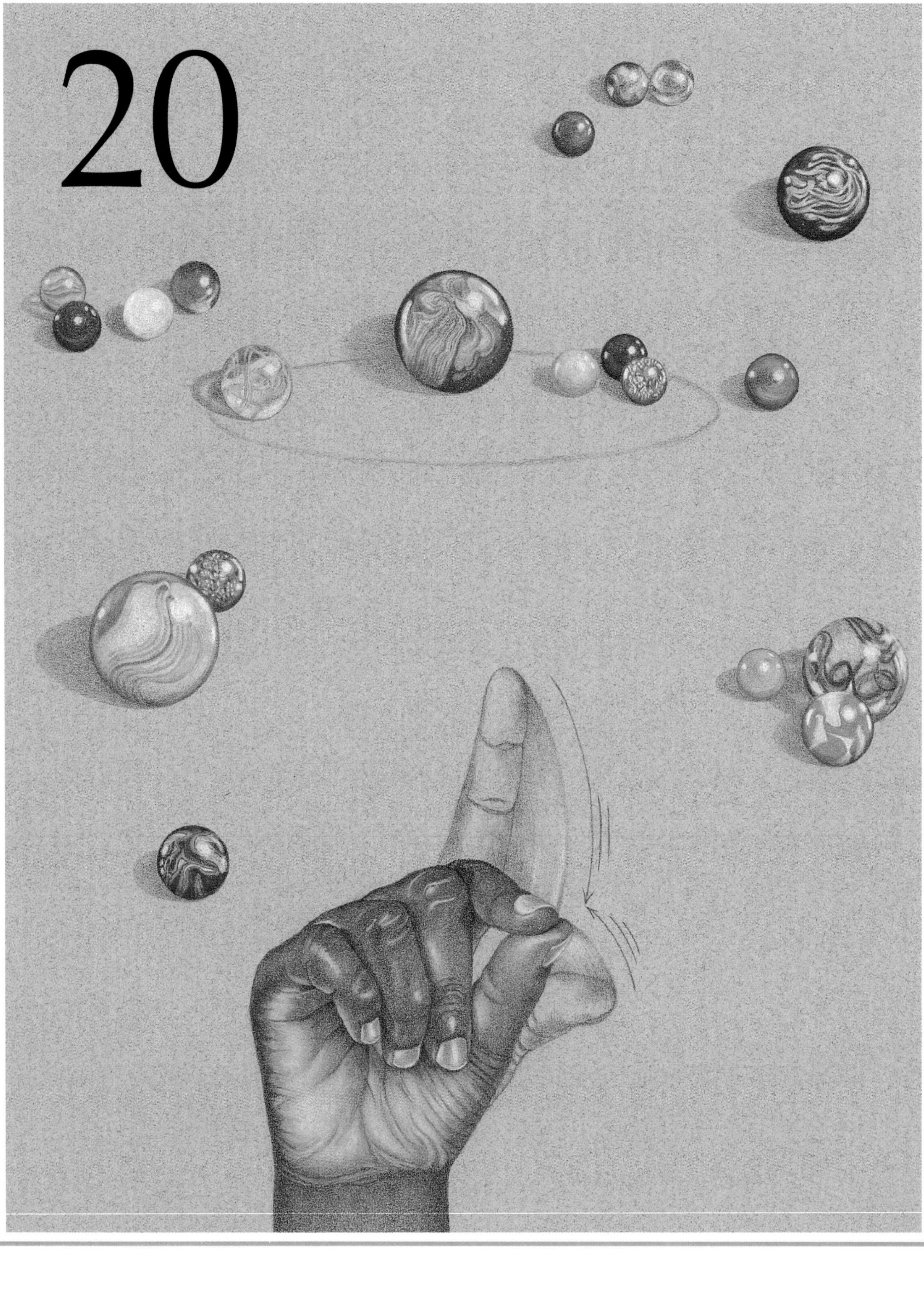

25

The images for the toys and objects shown in the art are listed below:

1. Tin biplane (also shown on last page)
2. Handmade puppets
3. Wooden train
4. Butterflies: Adonis blue, monarch, purple spotted swallowtail, cloudless sulphur
5. Russian nesting dolls
6. Mexican coconut shell masks
7. Boats: includes tugboats, sailboat, rowboat, fishing boats, and steamship
8. Wooden geese folk art toy
9. Seashells, *clockwise from lower left:* limpet, Doris harp shell, banded land snail, spindle tibia, royal cloak scallop, periwinkle, starfish, sea urchin, Episcopal miter
10. Plastic dinosaurs resemble the following, *clockwise from lower left:* Stegosaurus, Monoclonius, Triceratops, Allosaurus, Diplodocus, Styracosaurus, Maiasaura, Stegosaurus, Ankylosaurus, and Plateosaurus
11. Dolls from around the world, including handmade and antique American dolls and dolls from East India, *upper left;* Russia, *right foreground;* and Japan, *second from bottom right*
12. Flowers, *clockwise from lower left:* zinnia, false sunflower, Queen Anne's lace, purple cone-flower, zinnia; *near number twelve,* garden oregano; *below,* dahlia, two cosmos, aster, gloriosa daisy, and cosmos

13. Stuffed animals, including old, new, and handmade animals
14. Plastic and metal windup toys
15. Balloons
16. Vehicles: includes T-bird, drag-racing car, police cruiser, fire truck, tin touring car, racing cars, buses, backhoe, taxi, flatbed truck, and dump truck
17. Hand-painted wooden toy soldiers
18. Wooden blocks
19. Feathers: includes guinea hen, seagull, pheasant, and parrot
20. Glass marbles
25. Origami cranes
50. Marine fish, *clockwise from lower left:* 2 Cuban hogfish, 1 regal tang, 5 blue-striped snappers, 2 common clownfish, 3 cleaner wrasses, 1 harlequin sweetlips, 5 royal grammas, 3 Alexandria groupers, 4 pennant butterflyfish; *center:* 1 Garibaldi damselfish; *counterclockwise from lower right:* 1 beaked leatherjacket, 2 common clownfish, 3 yellow tangs, 2 humbug damselfish, 1 adult and 1 juvenile Gaimard's wrasse (also called clown wrasse), 6 blue damselfish, 4 gray mullets, 2 royal grammas, and 1 spotted trunkfish
75. Ceramic, glass, and plastic beads
100. Plastic Noah's ark: 98 animals plus Noah and his wife

The front cover shows the handshapes for the numbers 1, 2, and 3, with one jumping folk doll, two tops, and three oak leaves; the back cover shows the handshape for the number 4 with four butterflies, and the title page shows the handshape for the number 5 and five crayons.

Acknowledgments

I thank the following people for their help and support:

Everyone at St. Mary's School for the Deaf in Buffalo, New York, especially
Dr. David R. Updegraff; Jean Roeder; Cheryl Weigand; Veronica Barrera;
Jessica Czamara; Alex Dailey; Joshua Lloyd Davis; Shaneice Doyle; Ricky Eriksen;
Tyrone Ervin; Sarah Flowers; Minnie Frank; David Huff; Michael Lumley, Jr.;
Shawn Moore; Brandon J. Pitts; Chaynna Powell; Alex Shepard; Kadie Tower;
Dmitry Tsitsyala; and Valencia Williams.

From the seacoast, thanks to Brian Catapang; Kevin Catapang; Lauren Cooper;
Anna-Claire Pierce; Caitlin Pierce.

And finally, for loaning and/or making many of the toys and objects, thanks to
Sue Antal; Penny Brewster; Brian and Paulette Chernack; Kathy Cooper;
Nancy R. Davison; Michelle Dionetti; John Garand; Jamie Houtz; Mariah Houtz;
Carol Lucha-Burns; Jane MacLean; Sue Poulin; Nancy Rankin; Barbara Simpson;
Peg Stafford; John Stephenson; Harvey Wheeler; River Place, York, Maine;
and G. Willikers Toys, Portsmouth, New Hampshire.

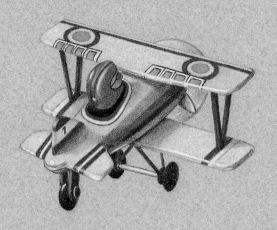